25 Super Sight Word Songs & Mini-Books

Joan Mancini

New York • Toronto • London • Auckland • Sydney
Mexico City • New Delhi • Hong Kong • Buenos Aires

Teaching *Resources*

✦ ✦ · **Dedication** · ✦ ✦

*To Nick and Stefanie, and all of the wonderful kids
who have inspired me to create in the classroom.*

Edited by Immacula A. Rhodes

Cover design by Maria Lilja

Interior design by Sydney Wright

Illustrations by Maxie Chambliss

ISBN–13: 978-0-545-10582-8
ISBN–10: 0-545-10582-X

Contents

Songs
★ ★ ★ ★ ★ ★

Introduction

Welcome to *25 Super Sight Word Songs & Mini-Books*, a delightful collection of songs and activities that make sight word lessons enjoyable and effective! The songs—set to familiar, easy-to-learn tunes—add a fun element to connecting the spellings to pronunciations of high-frequency words, while the mini-books give children practice in reading, writing, and using the words in context.

When I began teaching Kindergarten, I observed a teaching partner using songs to teach color words. I borrowed her materials to use with my students and I noticed that, through rhythm and music, the children learned to spell words such as *orange* and *purple*. So why not use this powerful teaching tool with important sight words, such as *the* and *like*? This prompted me to explore resources that would help incorporate music into my sight word lessons, but I could not find any songs! It was then that I set out on a mission to develop songs that could help children learn to read and spell sight words.

Many experts have indicated that context is an important key in teaching sight words, especially since a large number of these words are abstract and hard to teach in isolation. Based on this knowledge, I decided to include letter-by-letter spellings of targeted words in my songs, as well as a child-friendly and appropriate context for using the words. When singing the songs with my class, I noticed that many children who had previously been confused by sight words, such as the pronouns *she* and *he*, began to use the words correctly after hearing them incorporated in a way that demonstrated their use in context (for instance, *she* is a girl and *he* is a boy).

I also noticed that many of my shy students—in particular, those who were reluctant to speak up in class—readily began to sing along with the songs and enjoyed themselves in doing so. In addition, my English Language Learners, who were typically quiet in class, quickly joined in to sing the "silly songs." As noted by many experts, I found that music truly is an effective tool in engaging students and facilitating learning, while also lowering the affective filter in the classroom.

The materials in this resource make teaching sight words fun and easy. Each lesson includes a reproducible song sheet and mini-book along with an accompanying song on CD. On the following pages, you'll find directions for assembling and using the mini-books, teaching tips, and extension activities designed to engage students through multiple modalities. With minimal preparation, the songs and activities can be used right away, and they support the Mid-continent Research for Education and Learning (McREL) national and state standards for Language Arts. In addition, the mini-books serve as an instant tool to promote home-school connections—children will love using their books to share and sing the songs with their families!

The efficacy of conquering difficult concepts, such as learning to spell and read tricky words like *said* and *because*, can spill over and have a positive impact on other areas of learning. My goal for creating *25 Super Sight Word Songs & Mini-Books* is to provide a fun, motivating way to help children learn important skills and encourage them to become engaged, confident, lifelong learners. As you enjoy this resource with your students, remember—when teaching is fun, so is learning!

How to Use This Book

The lessons in *25 Super Sight Word Songs & Mini-Books* focus on teaching 35 specific high-frequency words. The songs and mini-books provide opportunities to teach and reinforce these important sight words through spelling, reading, writing, and rhythm activities. You can use the lessons and materials in whatever way or order that best suits your students. They can easily be used with individual children or student pairs, as well as small groups or the whole class.

What's Inside?

This collection includes a unit for each of the 25 songs, tips for using the materials to teach sight words, and extension activities to further support and strengthen children's learning. Here's an overview of what you'll find, along with suggestions for use.

* **Song Sheets:** This reproducible page includes the song title, tune, and lyrics to the sight word song. When introducing or singing the song, you can display the song sheet and track the words to help children make the connection between the spoken and written word.

* **Mini-Books:** Each lesson includes an easy-to-make, reproducible mini-book that gives children multiple opportunities to spell and write the target sight word (or words). They simply write the missing word on the blank lines to complete the sentences on each page. Since the mini-books repeat the song in a different format, children can refer to the song sheet to check their work. Children can also personalize most of the mini-books by adding their own drawings, which helps boost comprehension.

* **Music CD:** The lively performances on this CD make the sight word songs come alive! Children can sing along as they track the words to the songs in their mini-books or on a copy of the song sheet.

Introducing the Songs

Teaching the songs in this collection is quite easy! Before playing the song on CD, teach the lyrics to children first. You can display an enlarged copy of the song sheet and then use a "my turn, your turn" format to introduce the song by reading each line aloud and having children repeat it. After children have become familiar with the words, play the song and invite them to sing along. By pre-teaching the lyrics, you'll find that children will be ready to join right in when the music begins! Finally, follow up a few rounds of singing by having children complete the mini-book. This additional learning tool provides just the right reinforcement children need to read, write, and use the target word in context.

Making the Mini-Books

Making the books is quick and simple—just follow these three easy steps:

1. Make a copy of the mini-book pages on 8-1/2- by 11-inch paper.

2. Cut the pages apart along the dotted line.

3. Sequence and staple the pages together along the left side.

Teaching Tips

These useful tips will help you get the most from the song sheets, mini-books, and songs.

* Make an enlarged copy of the song sheet to display when introducing the sight word song. As you teach each line, track the text to help children make the connection between the spoken and written word. Or, if desired, copy the page onto a transparency and display it on an overhead projector to use with children.

* As you come to each target word in the song, use a highlighter pen to mark that word. You might distribute copies of the song sheet to children and have them highlight the words on their copies, too.

* After children become familiar with the song, cover the sight word where ever it appears on the song sheet. Then have children fill in the missing word when they come to it. Alternatively, you might cover the word spellings.

* Challenge children to clap each time they sing the target word—or have them substitute a clap for the word. They might even clap out the syllable count for the word.

* To add interest, invite children to hum the words as they follow along on the song sheet. Then, when they reach the target word, have them sing it aloud.

* Before beginning your lesson for a particular sight word, make a mini-book for that word to use as a model for children. If desired, enlarge copies of the pages, assemble the book, and complete it by filling in the blanks and drawing pictures on the appropriate pages. You can use your sample to demonstrate how to make the mini-book, as well as to show children how to complete each page.

* Based on children's needs and abilities, have them assemble and complete the mini-books in pairs, small groups, or as a whole class. Review each page with children and invite them to color the pictures. Have them fill in the blanks and add illustrations to represent the text on the pages that have drawing boxes. If desired, you might work individually with each child to assess his or her knowledge of the sight word.

* After completing the mini-books, invite children to use them to sing the song. You can have children sing in small groups or as a class. You might also encourage them to share their books with reading buddies, friends, and family members. Interpersonal learners will especially enjoy teaching the songs and singing them with others.

25 Super Sight Word Songs & Mini-Books © 2009 by Joan Mancini, Scholastic Teaching Resources

Extension Activities

Reading experts may have different opinions about which sight words children need to know, but they all agree that children need to interact with these words in a variety of ways to really learn them. There are many engaging ways to incorporate music and other modalities into your sight word lessons. The following activities work extremely well for each sight word in this resource and can be used with small groups or as individual or partner activities in centers.

Sight Word Puzzles

Create these puzzles by tracing large stencils to spell out the word on a half-sheet of 8 ½- by 11-inch paper. Or use your computer's word art program to create an enlarged sample of the word. Then laminate the page, puzzle-cut it into several pieces, and put the pieces in a large envelope labeled with the target word. Place the puzzles in a center for children to assemble, or invite them to use the puzzles when they have a few extra minutes to fill between activities. If desired, let children make their own word puzzles to share with family and friends.

Creative Word Collage

Copy a class quantity of an enlarged sight word as described in Sight Word Puzzles (above). Distribute the copies to children along with sheets of colored construction paper. Have them cut a loose outline around the word, glue it to the center of their paper, and then print the sight word in each corner of their paper. Next challenge children to use the space above, under, and around the cutout to write as many sentences with the word as they can. If children have difficulty coming up with sentences, they might copy a sentence or two from their sight word mini-book. Finally, invite them to add illustrations to go with their sentences.

Perfect Pointers

Have children make pointers to use when reading specific sight words. To begin, cut plain index cards into ¾- by 3-inch strips, cutting two strips for each child. Print the target word on each strip, using a capital letter to begin the word. Then invite children to color their two word strips, cut them out (by cutting around the shape of the words), and glue one to each side of a wide craft stick making sure the strips are glued to the same end of the stick. To use, have children search print around the room to find the sight word that's on their pointer. Whenever they find the word, have them point it out. They can also use their pointers to identify the word in their mini-books as they sing the song!

Conga Line Chant

Invite children to use their pointers (see Perfect Pointers, above) to signal the use of the sight word in this fun conga-line activity. First, have children form a straight line, pointers in hand. Then begin an upbeat conga-like rhythmic chant in which you can incorporate the spelling and pronunciation of the sight word, such as "S-h-e spells she!" Ask children to raise their pointers each time they say the target word. The combination of rhythm and movement is helpful in embedding the spelling-to-word relationship in children's memory. As you work with other words, you might alter the activity by using a different rhythm or movement, such as marching or hopping. This activity is sure to be a hit with your kinesthetic learners!

Jigsaw Sight Words

These jigsaw puzzles are great for visual-spatial learners! For this activity, you'll need small, blank, precut jigsaw puzzle frames (available from teacher supply and craft stores). To prepare, print a single sight word on the front of each puzzle. Take each puzzle apart and put the pieces in an envelope labeled with the sight word. To keep the pieces from getting mixed up with other puzzles, write the sight word on the back of each piece for that word. Then place the puzzles in a center for children to assemble. After completing each puzzle, children can write the word several times on paper or write sentences with the word.

Glitter-Glue Words

Create tactile word cards for children to use in word recognition activities. Simply write different sight words—in large print—on a supply of 3- by 5-inch index cards. Invite children to trace the words with glitter glue. After the glue dries, post the words around the room. Then give children paper and pencil attached to clipboards and challenge them to find the word cards. Each time they locate one, ask them to say (or sing) the word, trace it with their fingers, and then write it on paper.

Mystery Word

Invite partners to use the glitter-glue word cards (above) to play this guessing game. To begin, blindfold one of the children. Then have the child's partner lead that child to a glitter-glue word card and place his or her hand on the card. Ask the blindfolded child to carefully trace and retrace the letters on the card to try to figure out the mystery word. After guessing, remove the blindfold and let the child check his or her answer. Not only does this activity reinforce tactile learning, it also encourages teamwork!

Listen and Learn

Place the music CD, a CD player, several student magnet boards, and magnetic letters in a listening center. Then invite two or three children at a time to listen to the songs. Challenge them to use the letters to spell out each song's target word on their magnet board. As a variation, provide small whiteboards and wipe-off pens for children to use to write the word. Or fill large zippered plastic bags with hair gel, seal the bags, and have children use these as "magic boards" to write the words on. By incorporating a variety of modalities in this activity, children learn and have fun at the same time!

Magic Bumpy Words

For this "magical" activity, you'll need to color a supply of rock salt (available in the baking section of grocery stores). To do this, pour the salt into a zippered plastic bag, add a few

25 Super Sight Word Songs & Mini-Books © 2009 by Joan Mancini, Scholastic Teaching Resources drops of food coloring, seal the bag, and shake until the salt is colored. Afterwards, use a silver permanent marker to write the sight words on half-sheets of dark blue or black construction paper. Distribute the pages and ask children to trace their word with liquid glue. Next have them sprinkle the colored salt onto their paper and then shake off the loose salt into a container. As the salt falls off, the sight word will "magically" appear in color on the paper! After the glue dries, you might spray the projects with a craft fixative spray to help keep the "bumpy" words from falling off.

Multi-Sensory Sight Words

Here's another fun, multi-modal activity to help children learn sight words! Working with a group of six or fewer, have children spread out around a large table. Squeeze a small mound of unscented shaving cream for sensitive skin on the table in front of each child (check for allergies or skin sensitivity before beginning the activity). Then ask children to spread their shaving cream to form a rectangular shape. Next, invite them to choose a sight word from the word wall and then use their finger to write the word in their shaving cream. To erase, children simply smooth out the cream, and they're ready to write the next word. As children write their word, invite them to sing the song to add an auditory component to this visual and tactile activity.

Sight Word Stickers

At the beginning of your sight word lesson, write the target word on an adhesive-backed label or sticker for each child. Then, at the end of the school day, let children wear their stickers home and use them to "teach" the sight word to their family members. The next day—or later in the week—you might assess children to see if they can read or write the sight word from memory. If desired, you can give points to individuals or the entire class to reward them for learning the sight word. After collecting a specified number of points, let children choose a reward, such as extra time to do a favorite activity, a special snack, or free choice time.

Shapely Sight Words

Pass out play dough and let children use it to shape the letters needed to spell different sight words. Or provide copies of the words spelled in large print on half-sheets of paper and have children form play dough letters to match the letters in the words. If desired, pair up children and encourage each child to spell out a specified sight word with play dough. When finished, have children challenge their partners to look at the word, spell it, and then name it.

Wiffle-Ball Words

This sight word game requires quick thinking! To prepare, use a permanent marker to write several different sight words on a plastic Wiffle ball. Then have the class sit in a circle. Explain to children that they will pass the ball quickly around the circle, as in a game of hot potato. As they catch the ball, they must read a word on it before passing it to the next child. Each child should find a word that has not already been named by another player. If a word is repeated, or all the words have been named, start the game over.

Sight Word Surprise Spheres

Use 12 inexpensive, solid white ping-pong balls for this activity. First, use a permanent marker to write a different sight word on each ball. Then place the balls in a paper bag and seat children in a circle. Ask one child at a time to draw a ball from the bag, read aloud the word on the ball, and show the word to the group. Then have the child return the ball and pass the bag to the next child. For fun, you can keep count of how many times each word is pulled from the bag during a round of play. Or you might list all the words and then check off each one as it is drawn from the bag. In this version, have children continue play until all of the words have been checked off. For another variation, write each of the sight words on two balls. Then have children keep the ball they remove from the bag. After the bag has been passed around the circle, ask children to find the player who has the same sight word as theirs.

Home-School Connection

Send a letter home with children to explain the purpose of the mini-books and encourage parent/family participation. Here's an example of what you might put in the letter:

> Dear Parents/Caregivers,
>
> Your child has created this special mini-book that contains words to a song that can help him or her learn the word *because*! Ask your child to sing the song to you while tracking the words in the book. Then join in and sing along to share the fun and learning! Remember, each time your child reads the book or sings the song with you, he or she is getting important practice in reading and spelling skills. And—as a bonus—you'll be creating memorable moments with each other! So take some time with your child to sing, learn, and enjoy!

Connections to the Language Arts Standards

Mid-continent Research for Education and Learning (McREL), a nationally recognized, nonprofit organization, has compiled and evaluated national and state standards, and proposed what teachers should provide for their students to grow proficient in language arts, among other curriculum areas. The activities in this book support these standards for grades K–2 in the following areas:

Reading

- Uses mental images based on pictures and print to aid in comprehension of text
- Uses meaning clues to aid comprehension and make predictions about content
- Uses basic elements of phonetic analysis to decode unknown words
- Understands level-appropriate sight words and vocabulary
- Reads aloud familiar text with fluency and expression
- Knows the main ideas or theme of a story
- Relates stories to personal experiences

Writing

- Spells high-frequency words
- Uses descriptive words to convey basic ideas
- Writes in complete sentences
- Uses different parts of speech in writing (nouns, verb, adjectives, adverbs)
- Uses capitalization in writing

Source: Kendall, J. S. and Marzano, R. J. (2004). *Content knowledge: A compendium of standards and benchmarks for K–12 education.* Aurora, CO: Mid-continent Research for Education and Learning. Online database: http://www.mcrel.org/standards-benchmarks/

A

(Sing to the tune of "Alouette")

A is a letter,
the very first letter.
A is a letter,
and it's a word, too.

Here's a hot dog in a bun.
I can only eat just one.
A means one.
A means one.
O-o-o-oh!

A is a letter,
the very first letter.
A is a letter,
and it's a word, too.

I have a big piece of cake.
Only one, for goodness sake.
A means one,
A means one.
O-o-o-oh!

A is a letter,
our very first letter.
A is a letter,
and it's a word, too.

Page | 2 A   25 Super Sight Word Songs & Mini-Books © 2009 by Joan Mancini, Scholastic Teaching Resources

A

(Sing to the tune of "Alouette")

by _____

A is _____ letter,

the very first letter.

A is _____ letter,

and it's _____ word, too.

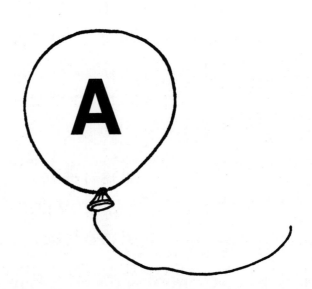

1

Here's _____ hot dog in _____ bun.

I can only eat just one.

A means one.

A means one.

O-o-o-oh!

A is _____ letter,

the very first letter.

A is _____ letter,

and it's _____ word, too.

I have _____ big piece of cake.

Only one, for goodness sake.

A means one,

A means one.

O-o-o-oh!

A is _____ letter,

our very first letter.

A is _____ letter,

and it's _____ word, too.

And

(Sing to the tune of "Are You Sleeping?")

A-n-d, *and.*
A-n-d, *and.*
I can spell *and.*
I can spell *and.*

One and one makes two.
I spell *and,* can you?
A-n-d,
a-n-d.

A-n-d, *and.*
A-n-d, *and.*
I can spell *and.*
I can spell *and.*

And means things together,
like rain and cloudy weather.
A-n-d,
a-n-d.

25 Super Sight Word Songs & Mini-Books © 2009 by Joan Mancini, Scholastic Teaching Resources

And

(Sing to the tune of "Are You Sleeping?")

by _____

A-n-d, _____.

A-n-d, _____.

I can spell _____.

I can spell _____.

1

One _____ one makes two.

I spell _____, can you?

A-n-d,

a-n-d.

A-n-d, _____.

A-n-d, _____.

I can spell _____.

I can spell _____.

And means things together,

like rain _____ cloudy weather.

A-n-d,

a-n-d.

Use *and* in a sentence. Then draw a picture.

_____

_____

Are

(Sing to the tune of "Do You Know the Muffin Man?")

A-r-e spells the word *are*,
the word *are*,
the word *are*,
A-r-e spells the word *are*,
a word we read each day.

Are you happy?
Are you sad?
Are you tired?
Are you mad?

Some questions start
with a-r-e,
a word we use each day.

A-r-e spells the word *are*,
the word *are*,
the word *are*,
A-r-e spells the word *are*,
a word we read each day!

Are

(Sing to the tune of "Do You Know the Muffin Man?")

by _____

A-r-e spells the word _____,

the word _____,

the word _____,

A-r-e spells the word _____,

a word we read each day.

_____ you happy?

_____ you sad?

_____ you tired?

_____ you mad?

Some questions start

with a-r-e,

a word we use each day.

A-r-e spells the word _____,

the word _____,

the word _____,

A-r-e spells the word _____,

a word we read each day.

Because

(Sing to the tune of "She'll Be Coming 'Round the Mountain")

B-e-c-a-u-s-e spells *because*.
B-e-c-a-u-s-e spells *because*.

Why do I eat?
Because I'm hungry.
Why do I drink?
Because I'm thirsty.
When we answer why,
we use the word *because*.

B-e-c-a-u-s-e spells *because*.
B-e-c-a-u-s-e spells *because*.

Why do I smile?
Because I'm happy.
Why do I laugh?
Because I'm silly.
When we answer why,
we use the word *because*.

Because

(Sing to the tune of "She'll Be Coming 'Round the Mountain")

by _____

B-e-c-a-u-s-e spells _____.

B-e-c-a-u-s-e spells _____.

because

Why do I eat?

_____ I'm hungry.

Why do I drink?

_____ I'm thirsty.

When we answer why,

we use the word _____.

2

B-e-c-a-u-s-e spells _____.

B-e-c-a-u-s-e spells _____.

3

Why do I smile?

_____ I'm happy.

Why do I laugh?

_____ I'm silly.

When we answer why,

we use the word _____.

4

Use *because* in a sentence. Then draw a picture.

_____

_____

5

Come and Some

(Sing to the tune of "Row, Row, Row Your Boat")

C-o-m-e, *come*,
come play ball with me.
C-o-m-e, *come*,
come and climb a tree.

Change the *c* to *s*.
Then *come* turns into *some*.
Change the *c* to *s*.
And *come* turns into *some*.

S-o-m-e, *some*,
Some kids are having fun.
S-o-m-e, *some*,
Some means more than one!

Come and Some

(Sing to the tune of "Row, Row, Row Your Boat")

by _____

C-o-m-e, _____,

come play ball with me.

C-o-m-e, _____,

_____ and climb a tree.

2

Change the *c* to *s*.

Then *come* turns into *some*.

Change the *c* to *s*.

And _____ turns into _____.

3

S-o-m-e, _____,

_____ kids are having fun.

4

S-o-m-e, _____,

_____ means more than one!

5

Could, Would, and Should

(Sing to the tune of "Bingo")

Three tricky words that we can spell—
The first one goes like this now:
c-o-u-l-d, *could*,
c-o-u-l-d, *could*,
c-o-u-l-d, *could*.
That's how we spell the word *could*.

Let's change the *c* to *w*
to make a brand new word, now:
w-o-u-l-d, *would*,
w-o-u-l-d, *would*,
w-o-u-l-d, *would*.
That's how we spell the word *would*.

Let's turn *would* into the word *should*
by adding two new letters:
s-h-o-u-l-d, *should*,
s-h-o-u-l-d, *should*,
s-h-o-u-l-d, *should*.
That's how we spell the word *should*.

Three tricky words that we can spell—
and each one goes like this, now:
c-o-u-l-d, *could*,
w-o-u-l-d, *would*,
s-h-o-u-l-d, *should*.
We've spelled *could*, *would*, and *should*, Yay!

Could, Would, and Should

(Sing to the tune of "Bingo")

by _____

Three tricky words that we can spell—

The first one goes like this now:

c-o-u-l-d, _____,

c-o-u-l-d, _____,

c-o-u-l-d, _____.

That's how we spell the word _____.

Let's change the *c* to *w*

to make a brand new word, now:

w-o-u-l-d, _____,

w-o-u-l-d, _____,

w-o-u-l-d, _____.

That's how we spell the word _____.

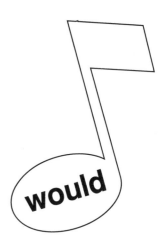

2

Let's turn *would* into the word *should*

by adding two new letters:

s-h-o-u-l-d, _____,

s-h-o-u-l-d, _____,

s-h-o-u-l-d, _____.

That's how we spell the word _____.

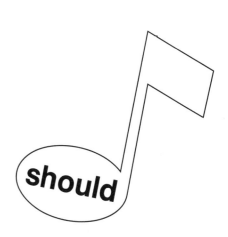

3

Three tricky words that we can spell—

and each one goes like this, now:

c-o-u-l-d, _____,

w-o-u-l-d, _____,

s-h-o-u-l-d, _____,

We've spelled _____,

_____, and _____, Yay!

could

would

should

4

- -

Write each word on the line.

could _____

would _____

should _____

Use one of the words in a sentence.

_____

_____

5

For and Four

(Sing to the tune of "Yankee Doodle")

F-o-r spells the word *for*.
F-o-r has three letters.
But number *four*
has more letters—
f-o-u-r, the number: 4!

F-o-r spells the word *for*.
I made toast for my mother.
F-o-r spells the word *for*.
I made lunch for my brother.

F-o-r spells the word *for*.
F-o-r has three letters.
But number *four*
has more letters—
f-o-u-r, the number: 4!

F-o-u-r—number 4.
I have four packs of crayons.
F-o-u-r—number 4.
I shared them with four friends.

For and Four

(Sing to the tune of "Yankee Doodle")

by _____

F-o-r spells the word _____.

F-o-r has three letters.

But number _____

has more letters—

f-o-u-r, the number: 4!

1

F-o-r spells the word _____.

I made toast _____ my mother.

2

F-o-r spells the word _____.

I made lunch _____ my brother.

3

F-o-r spells the word _____.

F-o-r has three letters.

But number _____

has more letters—

f-o-u-r, the number: 4!

F-o-u-r—number 4.

I have _____ packs of crayons.

F-o-u-r—number 4.

I shared them with _____ friends.

6

Write each word on the line.

for _____

four _____

Use one of the words in a sentence.

7

Have

(Sing to the tune of "On Top of Old Smoky")

H-a-v-e spells *have*,
A four-letter word.
It starts with the *h* sound,
Like *hot*, *hand*, and *heard*.

H-a-v-e spells *have*,
A word we all know.
I have a cool cap here.
I have balls to throw.

H-a-v-e spells *have*,
A word we all use.
I have a new glove, now.
I have some new shoes!

H-a-v-e spells *have*.
I have lots of friends.
I'll have lots of fun 'til
Our baseball game ends!

Have

(Sing to the tune of "On Top of Old Smoky")

by _____

H-a-v-e spells _____,

A four-letter word.

It starts with the *h* sound,

Like *hot*, *hand*, and *heard*.

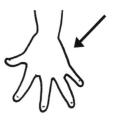

1

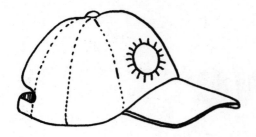

H-a-v-e spells _____,

A word we all know.

I _____ a cool cap here.

I _____ balls to throw.

2

H-a-v-e spells _____,

A word we all use.

I _____ a new glove, now.

I _____ some new shoes!

3

H-a-v-e spells _____.

I _____ lots of friends.

I'll _____ lots of fun 'til

Our baseball game ends!

Use *have* in a sentence. Then draw a picture.

_____

_____

He

(Sing to the tune of "Mary Had a Little Lamb")

H-e spells the small word *he*,
small word *he*, small word *he*.
H-e spells the small word *he*.
Yes, h-e means a boy.

He likes to do what he enjoys,
play with toys, make some noise.
He likes to do what he enjoys,
and h-e means a boy.

H-e spells the small word *he*,
small word *he*, small word *he*.
H-e spells the small word *he*.
Yes, h-e means a boy.

He

(Sing to the tune of "Mary Had a Little Lamb")

by _____

H-e spells the small word _____,

small word _____, small word _____.

H-e spells the small word _____.

Yes, h-e means a boy.

1

_____ likes to do what _____ enjoys,

play with toys, make some noise.

_____ likes to do what _____ enjoys,

and h-e means a boy.

2

H-e spells the small word _____,

small word _____, small word _____.

H-e spells the small word _____.

Yes, h-e means a boy.

3

Here and There

(Sing to the tune of "Skip to My Lou")

H-e-r-e spells the word *here*.
H-e-r-e spells the word *here*.
H-e-r-e spells the word *here*.
We are over here.

Add a *t* and you get *there*.
Add a *t* and you get *there*.
Add a *t* and you get *there*.
They are over there.

H-e-r-e spells the word *here*.
Add a *t* and you get *there*.
When you want to answer "Where?"
You can use *here* or *there*!

Here and There

(Sing to the tune of "Skip to My Lou")

by _____

H-e-r-e spells the word _____.

H-e-r-e spells the word _____.

H-e-r-e spells the word _____.

We are over _____.

there

Add a *t* and you get _____.

Add a *t* and you get _____.

Add a *t* and you get _____.

They are over _____.

2

H-e-r-e spells the word _____.

Add a *t* and you get _____.

When you want to answer "Where?"

You can use *here* or *there*!

3

I and Me

(Sing to the tune of "If You're Happy and You Know It")

Capital I spells *I*, and *I* is about me. M-e!
Capital I spells *I*, and *I* is about me. M-e!
Capital I is a letter, and a word that's about me.
Capital I spells *I*, and *I* is about me. M-e!

I use sentences all the time that start with *I*.
I like the stars. I like to watch them in the sky.
I means the same as *me*. It has one letter, look and see!
Capital I spells *I*, and *I* is about me. M-e!

Capital I spells *I*, and *I* is about me. M-e!
Capital I spells *I*, and *I* is about me. M-e!
Capital I is a letter, and a word that's about me.
Capital I spells *I*, and *I* is about me. M-e!

I and Me

(Sing to the tune of "If You're Happy and You Know It")

by _____

Capital I spells _____,

and _____ is about me. M-e!

Capital I spells _____,

and _____ is about me. M-e!

Capital I is a letter,

and a word that's about me.

Capital I spells _____,

and _____ is about me. M-e!

2

- -

_____ use sentences all the time

that start with _____.

_____ like the stars.

_____ like to watch them in the sky.

3

I means the same as _____,

It has one letter, look and see!

Capital I spells _____,

and *I* is about _____. M-e!

Capital I spells *I*,

and *I* is about _____. M-e!

Capital I spells *I*,

and *I* is about _____. M-e!

Capital I is a letter,

and a word that's about _____.

Capital I spells *I*,

and *I* is about _____. M-e!

Use *I* in a sentence.

_____

_____

Use *me* in a sentence.

_____

_____

Like

(Sing to the tune of "The Farmer in the Dell")

L-i-k-e spells *like*.
L-i-k-e spells *like*.
Hi, ho, did you know?
L-i-k-e spells *like*.

I like the color blue.
I like my new shoes, too.
Hi, ho, did you know?
L-i-k-e spells *like*.

L-i-k-e spells *like*.
L-i-k-e spells *like*.
Hi, ho, did you know?
L-i-k-e spells *like*.

I like to fly on planes.
I like to ride on trains. *(Choo-choo!)*
Hi, ho, did you know?
L-i-k-e spells *like*.

Like

(Sing to the tune of "The Farmer in the Dell")

by _____

L-i-k-e spells _____.

L-i-k-e spells _____.

Hi, ho, did you know?

L-i-k-e spells _____.

1

I _____ the color blue.

I _____ my new shoes, too.

Hi, ho, did you know?

L-i-k-e spells _____.

L-i-k-e spells _____.

L-i-k-e spells _____.

Hi, ho, did you know?

L-i-k-e spells _____.

I _____ to fly on planes.

I _____ to ride on trains.

Hi, ho, did you know?

L-i-k-e spells _____.

Use *like* in a sentence. Then draw a picture.

_____

_____

Little

(Sing to the tune of "Camptown Races")

L-i-t-t-l-e, *little, little*.
L-i-t-t-l-e is how we spell *little*.
I have a little cat. (*meow*)
She likes to sing like that. (*meow*)
L-i-t-t-l-e is how we spell *little*.

L-i-t-t-l-e, *little, little*.
L-i-t-t-l-e is how we spell *little*.
My little puppy barks. (*woof-woof*)
I walk him in the park. (*woof-woof*)
L-i-t-t-l-e is how we spell *little*.

L-i-t-t-l-e, *little, little*.
L-i-t-t-l-e is how we spell *little*.
I saw a little frog (*ribbit*)
On a giant log. (*ribbit*)
L-i-t-t-l-e is how we spell *little*.

Little

(Sing to the tune of "Camptown Races")

by _____

L-i-t-t-l-e, _____, _____.

L-i-t-t-l-e is how we spell _____.

I have a _____ cat.

She likes to sing like that.

L-i-t-t-l-e is how we spell _____.

1

L-i-t-t-l-e, _____, _____.

L-i-t-t-l-e is how we spell _____.

My _____ puppy barks.

I walk him in the park.

L-i-t-t-l-e is how we spell _____.

L-i-t-t-l-e, _____, _____.

L-i-t-t-l-e is how we spell _____.

I saw a _____ frog

On a giant log.

L-i-t-t-l-e is how we spell _____.

My

(Sing to the tune of "Oh Where, Oh Where Has My Little Dog Gone?")

M-y, m-y spells the little word *my*.
M-y is such a small word.

My dog,
My cat,
My house,
My friends,
I use *my* all of the time.

M-y, m-y spells the little word *my*.
M-y is such a small word.

My eyes,
My nose,
My legs,
My toes,
I use *my* all of the time.

M-y, m-y spells the little word *my*.
M-y is such a small word.

My name,
My hat,
My game,
My bat,
Oh, my! I used *my* again!

My

(Sing to the tune of "Oh Where, Oh Where Has My Little Dog Gone?")

by _____

M-y, m-y spells the little word _____.

M-y is such a small word.

_____ dog,

_____ cat,

_____ house,

_____ friends,

I use _____ all of the time.

My arms!

M-y, m-y spells the little word _____.

M-y is such a small word.

_____ eyes,

_____ nose,

_____ legs,

_____ toes,

I use _____ all of the time.

M-y, m-y spells the little word _____.

M-y is such a small word.

_____ name,

_____ hat,

_____ game,

_____ bat,

Oh, my! I used _____ again!

Use *my* in a sentence. Then draw a picture.

_____

_____

Play

(Sing to the tune of "Ten Little Indians")

P-l-a-y spells *play*.
P-l-a-y spells *play*.
P-l-a-y spells *play*.
May I play with you?

I play with my dog.
I play with my brother.

I play with my friends.
I play with my mother.

I play by myself.
I play with others.
Play is what I do!

P-l-a-y spells *play*.
P-l-a-y spells *play*.
P-l-a-y spells *play*.
I like to play, don't you?

Play

(Sing to the tune of "Ten Little Indians")

by _____

P-l-a-y spells _____.

P-l-a-y spells _____.

P-l-a-y spells _____.

May I _____ with you?

I _____ with my dog.

I _____ with my brother.

I _____ with my friends.

I _____ with my mother.

I _____ by myself.

I _____ with others.

Play is what I do.

4

P-l-a-y spells _____.

P-l-a-y spells _____.

P-l-a-y spells _____.

I like to _____, don't you?

5

Said

(Sing to the tune of "Oh My Darlin' Clementine")

S-a-i-d,
s-a-i-d,
s-a-i-d
spells *said*.

Mother said it's time to wake up.
It's time to get out of my bed.

S-a-i-d,
s-a-i-d,
s-a-i-d
spells *said*.

Teacher said it's time to learn now.
It's time to think and use my head.

S-a-i-d,
s-a-i-d,
s-a-i-d
spells *said*.

Father said it's time for sleep now.
It's time for me to go to bed!

Said

(Sing to the tune of "Oh My Darlin' Clementine")

by _____

S-a-i-d,

s-a-i-d,

s-a-i-d

spells _____.

Mother _____ it's time to wake up.

It's time to get out of my bed.

S-a-i-d,

s-a-i-d,

s-a-i-d

spells _____.

Teacher _____ it's time to learn now.

It's time to think and use my head.

S-a-i-d,

s-a-i-d,

s-a-i-d

spells _____.

Father _____ it's time for sleep now.

It's time for me to go to bed!

Use *said* in a sentence. Then draw a picture.

_____

_____

Saw

(Sing to the tune of "Jingle Bells")

S-a-w,

s-a-w,

s-a-w

spells *saw*.

I saw a dog

bark at a frog

and make it hop away!

S-a-w,

s-a-w,

s-a-w

spells *saw*.

The dog saw me

behind a tree

and ran over to play!

Saw

(Sing to the tune of "Jingle Bells")

by _____

S-a-w,

s-a-w,

s-a-w

spells _____.

I _____ a dog

bark at a frog

and make it hop away!

S-a-w,

s-a-w,

s-a-w

spells _____ .

The dog _____ me

behind a tree

and ran over to play!

4

Use *saw* in a sentence. Then draw a picture.

5

See

(Sing to the tune of "Three Blind Mice")

S-e-e,

s-e-e.

I can spell *see.*

I can spell *see.*

I see my friends who are sitting by me.

I see the letters *A, B,* and *C.*

I see my teacher who's smiling at me.

S-e-e,

s-e-e.

S-e-e,

s-e-e.

I can read *see.*

I can write *see.*

I see the rainbow across the sky.

I see a cloud in the sky, so high.

I see the birds as they fly on by.

S-e-e,

s-e-e.

See

(Sing to the tune of "Three Blind Mice")

by _____

S-e-e,

s-e-e.

I can spell _____.

I can spell _____.

I _____ my friends who are sitting by me.

I _____ the letters *A*, *B*, and *C*.

2

I _____ my teacher who's smiling at me.

S-e-e,

s-e-e.

3

S-e-e,

s-e-e.

I can read _____.

I can write _____.

4

I _____ the rainbow across the sky.

I _____ a cloud in the sky, so high.

5

I _____ the birds as they fly on by.

S-e-e,

s-e-e.

Use *see* in a sentence. Then draw a picture.

She

(Sing to the tune of "Have You Ever Seen a Lassie?")

S-h-e spells *she*,
spells *she*, spells *she*.
S-h-e spells *she*,
the word for a girl.

She is my big sister.
She is my grandmother.
S-h-e spells *she*,
the word for a girl.

S-h-e spells *she*.
spells *she*, spells *she*.
S-h-e spells *she*,
the word for a girl.

She writes down the alphabet.
She helps feed the class pet.
S-h-e spells *she*,
the word for a girl.

She

(Sing to the tune of "Have You Ever Seen a Lassie?")

by _____

S-h-e spells _____,

spells *she*, spells _____.

S-h-e spells _____,

the word for a girl.

1

_____ is my big sister.

_____ is my grandmother.

S-h-e spells _____,

the word for a girl.

2

___

S-h-e spells _____,

spells *she*, spells _____.

S-h-e spells _____,

the word for a girl.

3

_____ writes down the alphabet.

_____ helps feed the class pet.

S-h-e spells _____,

the word for a girl.

4

- -

Use *she* in a sentence. Then draw a picture.

_____

_____

5

The

(Sing to the tune of "This Old Man")

T-h-e,
t-h-e,
that's how to spell *the*, you see.
We write *the* in sentences,
and read it in books, too.
I can spell *the*.
How about you?

T-h-e,
t-h-e,
a tricky word for you and me.
We read and write *the*
many times a day.
T-h-e,
hip-hip-hooray!

The

(Sing to the tune of "This Old Man")

by _____

T-h-e,

t-h-e,

that's how to spell _____, you see.

1

We write _____ in sentences,

and read it in books, too.

I can spell _____.

How about you?

T-h-e,

t-h-e,

a tricky word for you and me.

We read and write _____

many times a day.

T-h-e,

hip-hip-hooray!

4

Use *the* in a sentence. Then draw a picture.

_____

_____

5

To

(Sing to the tune of "Good Night, Ladies")

T-o spells *to*.
T-o spells *to*.
T-o spells *to*.
I like to sing to you!

I like to dance.
I like to play.
I like to clap
to music every day.

T-o spells *to*.
T-o spells *to*.
T-o spells *to*.
I like to sing to you!

To

(Sing to the tune of "Good Night, Ladies")

by _____

T-o spells _____.

T-o spells _____.

T-o spells _____.

I like to sing _____ you!

1

I like _____ dance.

I like _____ play.

2

I like _____ clap

_____ music every day.

3

T-o spells _____.

T-o spells _____.

T-o spells _____.

I like _____ sing _____ you!

Use *to* in a sentence. Then draw a picture.

Want

(Sing to the tune of "Twinkle, Twinkle, Little Star")

W-a-n-t spells *want*.
W-a-n-t spells *want*.
Do you want to play with me?
Do you want to climb a tree?
W-a-n-t spells *want*.
W-a-n-t spells *want*.

W-a-n-t spells *want*.
W-a-n-t spells *want*.
I want to sing this silly song.
I want my friends to sing along.
W-a-n-t spells *want*.
W-a-n-t spells *want*.

W-a-n-t spells *want*.
W-a-n-t spells *want*.
Want can be a tricky word.
Chant it, spell it, and be heard!
W-a-n-t spells *want*.
W-a-n-t spells *want*.

Want

(Sing to the tune of "Twinkle, Twinkle, Little Star")

by _____

W-a-n-t spells _____.

W-a-n-t spells _____.

Do you _____ to play with me?

Do you _____ to climb a tree?

W-a-n-t spells _____.

W-a-n-t spells _____.

1

W-a-n-t spells _____.

W-a-n-t spells _____.

I _____ to sing this silly song.

I _____ my friends to sing along.

W-a-n-t spells _____.

W-a-n-t spells _____.

2

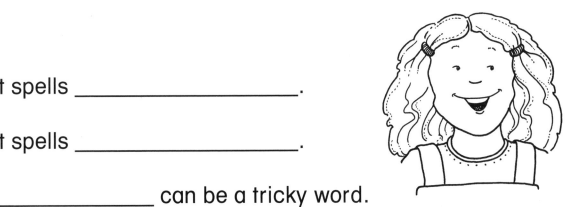

W-a-n-t spells _____.

W-a-n-t spells _____.

_____ can be a tricky word.

Chant it, spell it, and be heard!

W-a-n-t spells _____.

W-a-n-t spells _____.

3

Was

(Sing to the tune of "I'm a Little Teapot")

W-a-s spells the word *was*.
It starts with *w* and ends with *s*.
The ending sounds just like a *z*.
Was is tricky, can't you see?

W-a-s spells the word *was*.
Was rhymes with *fuzz* and *does* and *buzz*.
The last letter is an *s*, not *z*.
Was, you just can't fool smart me!

Was

(Sing to the tune of "I'm a Little Teapot")

by _____

W-a-s spells the word _____.

It starts with *w* and ends with *s*.

The ending sounds just like a *z*.

_____ is tricky, can't you see?

was

W-a-s spells the word _____.

_____ rhymes with *fuzz* and *does* and *buzz*.

The last letter is an *s*, not *z*.

_____, you just can't fool smart me!

Use *was* in a sentence. Then draw a picture.

_____

_____

Went

(Sing to the tune of "For He's a Jolly Good Fellow")

W-e-n-t spells *went*.
W-e-n-t spells *went*.
W-e-n-t spells *went*.
I went to school today!

I went to have some fun.
I got my schoolwork done.
W-e-n-t spells *went*.
I went to school today!

W-e-n-t spells *went*.
W-e-n-t spells *went*.
W-e-n-t spells *went*.
I went to school today!

We went to lunch on time!
I even found a dime.
W-e-n-t spells *went*.
I went to school today!

Went

(Sing to the tune of "For He's a Jolly Good Fellow")

by _____

W-e-n-t spells _____.

W-e-n-t spells _____.

W-e-n-t spells _____.

I _____ to school today!

1

I _____ to have some fun.

I got my schoolwork done.

W-e-n-t spells _____.

I _____ to school today!

W-e-n-t spells _____.

W-e-n-t spells _____.

W-e-n-t spells _____.

I _____ to school today!

We _____ to lunch on time!

I even found a dime.

W-e-n-t spells _____.

I _____ to school today!

Use *went* in a sentence. Then draw a picture.

Who, What, Where, When, and Why

(Sing to the tune of the military cadence "Sound Off")

Who, what, where, when, and *why*!
All are question words, oh my!

W-h-o, who do I see?
Who is that looking at me?

What is spelled w-h-a-t.
What song will you sing with me?

Sound off! Question words!
Sound off! I can spell!
Who, what, where, when, and *why*!

W-h-e-r-e spells *where*.
Where did I put my teddy bear?

When is spelled w-h-e-n.
When can I play with my friend?

W-h-y spells the word *why*.
Why can't I have more pumpkin pie?

Sound off! Question words!
Sound off! I can spell!
Who, what, where, when, and *why*!

Who, What, Where, When, and Why

(Sing to the tune of the
military cadence "Sound Off")

by _____

Who, what, where, when, and *why!*

All are question words, oh my!

W-h-o, _____ do I see?

_____ is that looking at me?

_____ is spelled w-h-a-t.

_____ song will you sing with me?

Sound off! Question words!

Sound off! I can spell!

Who, *what*, *where*, *when*, and *why*!

W-h-e-r-e spells _____.

_____ did I put my teddy bear?

_____ is spelled w-h-e-n.

_____ can I play with my friend?

W-h-y spells the word _____.

_____ can't I have more pumpkin pie?

Sound off! Question words!

Sound off! I can spell!

Who, what, where, when, and *why!*

Write each word on the line.

who _____

what _____

where _____

when _____

why _____